Give Save Spend with the Three Little Pigs

CLINT GREENLEAF
with ILLUSTRATIONS BY PHIL WILSON

www.pigsandbricks.com

Published by Pigs and Bricks LLC
Austin, Texas
www.pigsandbricks.com

Copyright ©2018 Clinton T. Greenleaf III

Distributed by Pigs and Bricks LLC
For ordering information or special discounts for bulk purchases, please contact
Pigs and Bricks at PO Box 92664, Austin, TX 78709.

Illustrations by Phil Wilson

Publisher's Cataloging-In-Publication Data
Greenleaf, Clinton T.
Give, Save, Spend with the Three Little Pigs / Clint Greenleaf; with illustrations by
Phil Wilson.—2nd ed.
p. : col. ill. ; cm.
Summary: The Three Little Pigs help you learn about money.
Interest age level: 004-006.
ISBN: 978-1-942148-03-6
1. Money—Juvenile literature. 2. Finance, Personal—Juvenile literature. 3. Swin—
Juvenile literature. 4. Money. 5. Finance, Personal. 6. Pigs. I. Wilson, Phil, 1948- II.
Title. III. Title: Give, save, spend with the Three Little Pigs
PZ7.G74 Gi 2014
[E]   2013945039

Part of the Tree Neutral® program, which offsets the number of trees consumed in
the production and printing of this book by taking proactive steps, such as planting
trees in direct proportion to the number of trees used: www.treeneutral.com

Printed in the United States of America on acid-free paper

17 18 19 20 21 22 10 9 8 7 6 5 4 3 2

Second Edition

To Susie, Abby, and Clint—
Thank you for always inspiring me!

$\mathcal{D}$o you remember the Three Little Pigs?

Not long ago, they lived in separate houses they had built—one made of straw, one made of sticks, and one made of bricks. The mean old Big Bad Wolf blew down the straw house and the stick house.

But the brick house was so strong, the Big Bad Wolf could not huff and puff and blow it down. So the two other Pigs moved into the brick house with their brother and were safe and sound.

But there was still trouble in the forest. Since the Big Bad Wolf could not blow down the Pigs' brick house, he decided to blow down the other animals' houses, one after another!

The animals were very upset.

"I have Wolf problems," said the deer. "I would like to have a strong house for my family."

"Me too!" said the squirrel.

"You're not the only ones!" said the raccoon. "My family would like a strong house so we can sleep all day without worrying about that Wolf."

Word spread through the forest that the Pigs had the strongest and safest house around. The other animals decided they needed strong brick homes of their own.

The animals visited the Pigs and asked them if they would build them their own brick houses. The animals even offered to pay them. The Three Little Pigs thought about it and decided they could help their friends and make money too.

The Pigs made some drawings to show the animals how they would build each house. The deer family became the Pigs' first customer!

The Pigs began construction on the deer family's house. They were careful to use strong bricks and windows, and they built the house just as they had promised. They took their time and followed the plans carefully.

Soon the house was finished. The deer family was now safe and warm, and they told the other animals how much they loved their Pig-built brick home. Now, everyone wanted a brick house!

As time passed, the Pigs built houses for many animals.
The Big Bad Wolf would not bother these animals ever again!

As the Pigs built more houses, they earned more and more money. They carefully kept track of the money they earned and how much they spent to build each home.

The Pigs sat down to count the money they had left over after paying the costs to build all the homes—this was their profit. Now they had to decide what to do with all the money they made!

"We work very hard," said the first Pig. "I think we should spend this money on things that are fun! I want to buy some new clothes, to go on vacation, and to buy a lot of ice cream."

"It would be fun to get a new playscape too," he said.

The second Pig said, "Fun things would be nice, but fun doesn't last long. I think we should give our money to help other animals. The fish need clean water. We could pay the beavers to clean the lake."

"And that crazy grasshopper gets hungry every winter—we could buy him some food with our money. It would be nice to help other animals."

"Giving is a wonderful idea, and spending is fun," said the
third Pig. "But I think we should put our money in the bank."

"It would be nice to save it for a rainy day, like if
we need to fix the roof or if there is an emergency."

The Pigs thought and thought and thought. Each idea was good, but which one should they choose? They all liked each idea.

Finally, the three Pigs decided that they didn't have to pick just one idea. Spending, giving, and saving were all good ideas. "We'll do all three!" they cheered.

The Pigs gathered the profit and divided the money into three equal piles: one for giving, one for saving, and one for spending.

And from that day forward, every time the
Three Little Pigs earned money, they split it
among their three banks.

Glossary

We used some big words in this book, so let's see what they all mean:

Costs: the money a business needs to spend to do its job.
Businesses want to keep costs as low as possible.

Give: when someone takes their own money and chooses to let
someone else have it.

Profit: the money that is left over after a business pays for all of its
costs. Businesses want to make a profit.

Save: when someone puts money into a bank to keep it safe and
let it grow.

Spend: when someone uses money to buy things they want or need.

Parents' Guide

I wrote this book to begin teaching my children about money in a fun way. The concept of give, save, spend has grown in popularity recently and is a great foundation for learning. I wanted to explain the concept to them in simple terms and make it an enjoyable process as well. Many parents who want to encourage their children to be responsible with money have struggled with the best way to do it. I hope this story can be a first step in your child's financial education.

As you read, you may want to teach other lessons or include other activities. Here are some ideas.

Discussion Questions

- What are some of the different ways people earn money and why?

- How do you earn money and how does the family give, save, and spend it?

- What is a business? Why did the Pigs start one?

- What does it mean to charge a fair price or do quality work?

Activities

- Set up three banks for your child (just like the Pigs did) and focus on giving money in increments that are easily divisible by three. (For more on this idea, see the next page.)

- Teach your child how to count money—it seems to be a dying art. Children love to play with coins; counting money is a great way to develop basic math skills.

- When choosing where to give money, involve your child in the decision and in actually giving the money—you don't want to force a cause on them or make them think that giving is a tax.

- Help your child set up a bank account and talk about the goal of putting money aside so that it can grow and be available for a rainy day. Ask the bank if they can send you monthly statements by mail—kids love to get mail and it will be a regular reminder that they are saving. (You might choose to subsidize the interest rate, as low rates might discourage a youngster.)

- Your parenting style will dictate how much you want to be involved in what your child buys. However, remember that it's much better for kids to make mistakes early on in their lives than as adults, so try to focus on giving your child first-hand experience rather than influencing every decision.

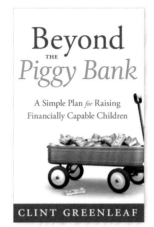

For a robust discussion of these topics, and many more, you can read my parents' guide on finances, *Beyond the Piggy Bank: A Simple Plan for Raising Financially Capable Children*. We've also developed a forum for you to share your best practices and questions with other parents. Please visit www.PigsandBricks.com for more info.

Piggy Bank Activity

(ages four to eight)

This bank-decorating project is a fun way to continue the give-save-spend discussion with your children and to generate excitement about the skills they learned from the Three Little Pigs. My wife and I bought each of our children three white ceramic piggy banks and an assortment of art supplies. The kids used their creativity to decorate each of their banks.

Your child's "Give" bank could be decorated with the name or symbol of your place of worship, or of a charity that is important to them.

The "Save" bank could feature a picture of a bank, the college that your child hopes to attend, or a big item, such as a car.

The "Spend" bank tends to be the most exciting. We've seen pigs decked out with drawings of candy, toys—most anything our children can imagine!

Encourage your children to use the banks and watch their money grow in ways that are responsible, thoughtful, and especially fun. To order your own piggy banks and find more detailed activity plans, visit www.PigsandBricks.com.